New Creation
A Youth Devotional

by Katy Newton Naas

New Creation © 2024 by Katy Newton Naas. All rights reserved. No portion of this book may be reproduced, stored in a retrieval system, or transmitted in any form or by any means, except for brief quotations in printed reviews, without prior permission from the author.

Scripture quotations are from The ESV® Bible (The Holy Bible, English Standard Version®), copyright © 2001 by Crossway, a publishing ministry of Good News Publishers. Used by permission. All rights reserved.

Published by HIS Books

ISBN: 979-8-9858468-8-1

I dedicate this devotional to my Lord and Savior, Jesus. I am so grateful that You didn't leave me in that mess of my old life. Thank You for never giving up on me and for making me new!

Introduction:
What Does It Mean to Be a Christian?

Let's face it: there are a lot of people in the world who call themselves Christians, but don't really know what the term means.

You've probably heard the expression, "They can talk the talk but can't walk the walk." This is true of many, unfortunately, who claim to be Christians.

Maybe they go to church. Maybe they prayed a prayer once, asking Jesus to forgive their sins and help them commit to Him. And that's good stuff – necessary stuff. But it's not all there is to it.

The problem is, a lot of people don't really know what should happen next.

So let's back up a step. Have you made that decision to follow Jesus? If not, let's talk about what that means and why it's the most important decision you will *ever* make.

Let's go way back – back to the very beginning, before the world ever existed, when there was only God. Before He ever took those six days to create the world and everything in it, He had already dreamed up *you*. Even way back then, He knew this world would one day need you in it. God is love, and He created you to love you. To have a real relationship with you. He planned your days out. He created your gifts and talents. He gave you strengths and weaknesses. And He made a place that only *you* can fulfill in His great plan for His kingdom.

But here's the problem: sin gets in the way. Sin is anything you do that goes against God. God is perfect. He has never sinned, and He cannot tolerate sin. He made humans with the ability to choose our words, thoughts, and actions…and many times, we choose *wrong*.

Read Romans 3:23 in your Bible. Write that verse here:

_____

_____

_____

_____

According to this verse, every person in this world has sinned against God in some way. That sin makes us lose the connection to God that He wants us to have. Sin cannot go unpunished.

God knew it was impossible for you to be perfect. He knew you would fall short over and over again. So, in His love and goodness, He made a plan to save you from that sin: He sent His Son, Jesus, to pay the penalty. Jesus lived a perfect life here in this world, then willingly gave His life as the payment for your sin. And because of His sacrifice, all you have to do is put your faith and trust in Him.

Read Romans 6:23 in your Bible. Write that verse here:

_____

_____

_____

_____

Notice the cost of sin? It's death. But the cost of the gift of Jesus? It's FREE. And all you have to do is accept it. When you do, your sins are forgiven. It's that simple.

So how do you accept it? That's simple, too. Read John 14:6 in your Bible. Write it here:

_____

_____

_____

_____

Notice what Jesus said: He is THE way, truth, and life. He's not just one *option* of how to get there. He is the *only way* to get there. You have to put your faith and trust in Him as your Savior.

So I'll ask you again: have you made that decision to follow Him? If you haven't, don't waste any more time. Start with a simple conversation with God. You don't have to use big, fancy words. You don't have to be at church, although you certainly can be. You can have this conversation at home, in your car, at your desk at school, or on the basketball court. He can hear you, no matter where you are.

When you start that conversation, begin by thanking Him for loving you, for having a plan for you, for sending Jesus to take the punishment you deserve. Tell Him you admit that you have done, said, and thought many wrong things in your life, and that you're sorry. Tell Him you realize how much you need Him, and ask Him to take your sins and your guilt away. Tell God that from now on, you want to stop trying to do everything *your* way and instead, you want to turn to His way.

If you had this conversation with God – whether it was right this moment, or years ago – congratulations! You have taken the first step in becoming a Christian. You are beginning the greatest journey life has to offer.

Throughout this devotional, we will walk this journey with Jesus together. We will look at what the Bible says about being a Christian and what that should look like in our lives. We will figure out how to use what the Bible says and apply it to our lives today.

It isn't a short, easy walk; sometimes, the road gets long, rough, and rocky. Some days will feel like you're on top of the world, but other days, you may feel like giving up. But one thing is sure: the journey will *always* be worth it.

So what are we waiting for? Let's start walking the walk!

Day One:
A New Creation

I've heard many people say they will "get right with God" someday, but first they have to stop [insert whatever sin here]. After they get it together, *then* they will go to church and start praying.

But here's what they don't realize: you don't have to try to become a "better person" before you come to God. He wants you right now, just as you are, no matter what messes you've made in your life. Just surrender yourself, flaws and all, and watch what He will do in your life.

He will take you as you are, right in the middle of your mess, but He refuses to leave you in it.

Read 2 Corinthians 5:16-17. Write those verses here:

_____

_____

_____

_____

If something has "passed away," it's gone. Dead. That means the old you – the one who lived without following Jesus – that person is gone. You are made new! Whatever sins you've committed up to this point, they're wiped clean in God's eyes. You get a do-over. A new start.

This doesn't mean you're automatically perfect. In fact, spoiler alert: you'll never be perfect. At least not here on earth. But it *does* mean you get to start living life the way God made you to.

It's going to take effort on your part. It means you're going to have to turn your back on the sin that used to be part of your daily life.

You can start small. List one or two things you do or say that need to "die" along with the old you. Even if you've been a Christian for a long time, I think we can all admit there are areas in our life that could use some cleaning up. What do you need to eliminate from your life? Is it gossip? Bad language? Bad or harmful habits? Where can you start?

_____

_____

_____

_____

Here's another thing: you don't have to try to eliminate these sins on your own. Yes, you have to make the effort. But God is ready to come alongside you and help you in your walk. Ask Him to help you stay strong and resist those old habits, whatever they may be. Write a short prayer to Him, asking Him to help you become the new creation He has in mind.

_____

_____

_____

_____

_____

_____

_____

_____

_____

_____

Day Two:
Born Again

Let's talk a little more today about the idea of being a new creation. In the last devotion, we looked at the idea of eliminating the sinful stuff from our daily walk. But there's more to the idea of being "made new" than just getting rid of the bad. Let's look at a conversation Jesus had to help us dive into this topic a little more.

As Jesus lived here on earth in His final years, word started to spread about Him. His teachings, His miracles – people were drawn to Him.

Not all of the attention was good. Many of the religious leaders at the time, the Pharisees, were jealous of the attention He was getting. But some of them couldn't help but be drawn to Him, too. One man, Nicodemus, came to Him at night, eager to talk to Him and find out more about who He was.

While they were talking, Jesus said something to Nicodemus that sounded so strange to him. Read John 3:3 and write it here:

_____

_____

_____

_____

Nicodemus didn't understand. How could anyone be born a second time? And Nicodemus was one of the Jewish people. Jewish people were God's chosen people. Didn't that mean they would automatically go to heaven when they died? That's what they had always been taught.

Jesus explained what He meant – being born again meant to be born of the Spirit of God. This means a new life, one where the Spirit leads.

Nicodemus still couldn't make sense of what Jesus said. That's when Jesus explained the most beautiful promise God has for us: that whoever believes in Him will have eternal life. Despite what Nicodemus had always been told, it wasn't about his performance at all – it was simply about believe in, trusting in, and clinging to Jesus for that salvation. It can't be earned. It's about choosing Jesus over the sin that once held power over us.

Jesus revealed His purpose to Nicodemus that night: He came into the world to save us all. He would be our rescue, our hope, our healing. God's promise of heaven still stands today, and He is offering it to you. All you have to do is believe in Jesus and be born again through Him.

It's like you're on trial for a crime, and the judge declares you guilty. But instead of handing you the life sentence, the judge lets someone else take the punishment for you. That would never happen in our world, would it? But that's exactly what Jesus did. He took the punishment we deserve and gave us the promise of heaven someday.

When you truly begin to understand what Jesus did and decide to live your life for Him, that's when you begin to understand the idea of being "born again." Read Ephesians 4:24. Write it here:

_____

_____

_____

_____

Jesus wants to work in you, helping you become the person He created you to be. The "new self" God has prepared for you is where you will find your true purpose, joy, and fulfillment. While your new self won't look exactly like anyone else's, one thing is sure: God designed your new self to be more like Jesus.

Write a short prayer to God, asking Him to help you truly understand the concept of being "born again". Ask Him to help you become that new person and walk in His purpose instead of your own.

_____

_____

Day Three:
The First Fruit of the Spirit

Okay, so the Bible says you're a new creation. What in the world does that mean? What does it look like?

You know it means letting go of old sins, old bad habits. You know it means being "born again" and becoming a new creation. But if you're letting go of those parts of your old identity, what should the "new you" look like?

Don't worry: the Bible gives us some pointers for that. It tells us in the book of Galatians that as Christians, we are called to bear fruit. You know how an apple tree produces apples? And a pear tree produces pears? Well, a Christian produces something called the Fruit of the Spirit. When you begin following Jesus, He sends the Holy Spirit to live inside you, helping you to produce the fruit that every Christian should have.

So what is that fruit? Read Galatians 5:22-23. Write those verses here:

_____

_____

_____

_____

*Note: We're going to break this verse down over the next several days, so you will have to refer back to it many times. This is really one of those verses that Christians should memorize, because it's important to remember the qualities you should have. Make it a point to read over it several times each day so it can start living in your mind.

Okay, so let's break it down, starting with the first fruit mentioned: *love*. "Love" might be one of the most misused words in the world. Lots of people just throw out the word without meaning it or really thinking about it, which makes it difficult to really define it or understand it. But Biblical love? It's sacrificial. It's giving up part of ourselves for the good of others. *It's not a feeling, it's an action.*

So ask yourself this: are you filled with love? Do you go out of your way to show love to the people in your path each day? And it's not even just talking about your best friends or your family – it's *all* people. Do you give up your time and your resources to give to others? Are you loving?

Most of us, if we're being honest with ourselves, can admit we could and should have more love for others. So if Biblical love is shown in action, make a plan. Who can you show love to today? And what can you do – what *specific* action can you do – in order to show it?

_____

_____

_____

_____

Loving others isn't always easy. And let's be real: some people flat out make it hard to love them. You won't love all people naturally – it takes the Holy Spirit working inside of you to help you love them. Write a short prayer to God, asking Him to help you and fill you with love for others in your life, even when it's difficult.

_____

_____

_____

_____

Day Four:
The Second Fruit of the Spirit

We spent yesterday talking about love and what that should look like in a Christian's life. Today, we're going to take a deeper look at that second fruit of the spirit, which was *joy*.

If you asked any random people to tell you what "joy" means, many would likely say it means "happy." And while they're sort of right, there's actually a lot more to it. "Happiness" is about your circumstances. When you get a good grade on a difficult assignment, you feel happy. When you spend time doing something fun with your best friend, you feel happy. It's all about what's going on in the moment.

Biblical joy is so much more than happy feelings. It's a lasting emotion. It has nothing to do with what's going on around you. It comes from the choice to trust God and believe in His promises, knowing that no matter what happens in our lives, we will always have His love. It fills us up even when life gets tough.

The Bible has a lot to say about joy. Read Proverbs 17:22 and write it here:

_____

_____

_____

_____

Notice what it compares a "joyful heart" to: it's like medicine. Medicine makes you feel better, right? That's what a joyful heart does, too.

Would people describe you as joyful? Do you try to stay positive and in a good mood most of the time, even when life doesn't feel so awesome?

If you struggle with this – and a lot of people do – one thing that helps is to focus on your blessings. If you think about all the things God has given you, you'll find you have a lot to be thankful for. Remember to include the little things we often taken for granted: things like food to eat, running water, soap, and a toothbrush. Taking time out of your day *every single day* to thank God can really help you go from feeling down and negative to feeling joyful.

From here on out, we will start some of our devotions by thanking God for something in your life. While it's good to thank Him over and over for your biggest blessings, like your family, I challenge you to try to think of something new every day to add to your list as well.

So let's start now! Write a short prayer to God, thanking Him for some of your many blessings.

_____

_____

_____

_____

Day Five:
The Third Fruit of the Spirit

Before we jump in with the third fruit today, let's start with a short prayer to God, thanking Him for the blessings on your heart today.

_____

_____

_____

Okay, back to the third fruit of the spirit: *peace*. There are actually different kinds of Biblical peace, and they're all important.

There is *peace with God*, which only comes when we know Jesus as our Savior. It's peace that comes from a relationship with Him.

There is also *inner peace*, which is a calmness inside. This peace also comes from God, and He gives it to us for whatever situation we need. When we feel confused, He can give us peace to guide us. When we feel hurt or angry, His peace can comfort us. When we are worried, His peace can soothe us and give us confidence.

Another kind of peace is *peace with others*. We all know how difficult it can be to get along with others. But with God's peace, it is actually possible. With God's help, we can avoid the arguing and fighting and drama that so often takes over at school or at even at home.

It is REALLY easy to get sucked in to drama. You have to make the effort to stay out of situations that steal your peace. Read Psalms 34:14 and write it here:

_____

_____

_____

The Bible orders us to turn away from evil and to seek peace. That means when you hear those around you talking badly about someone or trying to stir up trouble, you get away from the situation and talk to God, asking for His peace.

And yes, there will be times when you can't avoid conflict. Not everyone is always going to see eye-to-eye in every situation, and there will be times you disagree with others. But there are Biblical ways to deal with those issues that don't include fighting and drama. Ask God to help you confront those situations in a peaceful manner, having calm conversations instead of letting it escalate and get out of control.

Ask yourself some honest questions: Do you feel peace inside? Do you bring peace to situations? Do you stay out of the drama that everyone else wants to play into? Do you try to get along with the people in your life?

Talk to God about that peace that He offers, especially if your answer to any of the questions above was *no*. Write a short prayer asking Him to fill you with His peace, no matter what is going on around you.

_____

_____

_____

_____

Day Six:
The Fourth Fruit of the Spirit

What are you feeling thankful for today? Take a moment to write a quick prayer of thanks to God.

_____

_____

_____

_____

Today, we're looking at the fourth fruit of the spirit: *patience*. Having patience means you're able to tolerate annoyances without getting angry or upset.

This can be a tough one for sure. When everything is going right, it's pretty easy to be patient. But we all know people or things that test our patience regularly. Patience is a quality so many struggle with – even Christians. It's controlling yourself and not letting anger or frustration take over when someone else is annoying you, or moving way too slowly in front of you in the hallway, or asking questions that they should already know the answer to.

Are you patient with the people in your life? Even with "those people" – the ones in your class, or on your team, or siblings at home…the ones who sometimes make you feel like you're about to lose your mind? Write a short prayer asking God to help you and fill you with the patience you need.

_____

_____

_____

_____

There's a different kind of patience, too: being able to tolerate delays. In a world that moves so fast – a world where information and entertainment is at our fingertips instantly – it can be really difficult to wait for something. But while God is loving and answers our prayers, He doesn't always give us what we ask for immediately. Sometimes we won't see our prayers answered for days, weeks, months, or even years after we've asked Him. Part of being patient is learning to trust God's timing and waiting on Him.

When you're in a difficult situation, it's easy to get frustrated when God doesn't immediately pull you out of it. Read James 5:8 and write it here:

_____

_____

_____

_____

Remember, when you can't see an end in sight: be patient. His answer is coming. Trust Him, and in the meantime, look for what He can teach you in the situation.

Day Seven:
The Fifth Fruit of the Spirit

Be kind. It's a catch phrase you hear and see everywhere – on T-shirts, merchandise, in the media. Kindness is the fifth fruit of the spirit, and while most people probably feel they understand what kindness is, it's hard to define. According to the dictionary, being "kind" involves being friendly, generous, and considerate of others. These are all qualities of kindness, yet they don't fully explain it.

If you want to see kindness, study the life of Jesus. Look at the way He made people *feel*. When people had an encounter with Him, it left an impression – and not just because of His miracles.

Our world is desperate for that Jesus-style kind of kindness – the kind that shares uplifting words and gestures. The kind that doesn't tear others down, even enemies. The kind that is warm, loving, and leaves others wanting to be around it more.

Are you kind to others? Not just your friends or family, but *all* others? Like that kid who's always mean? Or the one who annoys you? When other people interact with you, are they left with good, warm feelings?

Really reflect on those questions. Talk to God about it, and ask Him to show you where you fall short in this area. Write a short prayer, asking Him to help you show Jesus-like kindness in all you say and do, even when it's not easy.

_____

_____

_____

_____

Jesus found small ways to share kindness. For example, a man with leprosy – a horrible skin condition that left its victim alone and isolated from others – approached him, begging for healing. Jesus could have healed him from a distance. But instead, he reached out and touched the man to heal him. This was a small kindness, because the man hadn't been able to get within six feet of another person since the disease struck. He chose touch – something he knew the man needed – to cleanse him. That's kindness!

What can you do to show kindness to someone today? It doesn't have to be a big, elaborate gesture, and it doesn't have to cost money or even much time. Make a plan to do something kind for just one person in your path today. Write it here.

_____

_____

_____

_____

Finally, read Ephesians 4:32. Write the verse here:

_____

_____

_____

_____

Work on committing this verse to memory.

Day Eight:
The Sixth Fruit of the Spirit

Let's start the day by giving thanks today. Write a short prayer to God, thanking Him for something that has happened in the last week.

_____

_____

_____

_____

Now, let's continue with the next fruit of the spirit on the list: *goodness*. The word "good" means *holy, pure, and righteous*. It means we're trying to be like God in what we do and say.

That's a tough one, isn't it? Because we already know we can't be perfect like God; He is good, but we are not. If we strive to be perfect, we set ourselves up to fail.

But that doesn't mean we can't be *better*. We can be honest with ourselves about our shortcomings and work on them. We can ask God for help in those areas we fall short. The thing is, struggles with sin are going to look different for everyone. Some will struggle with anger. Others will struggle with gossip. The trick is figuring out where your weaknesses are, and asking God to help you deal with them.

Take a moment to talk to God about this. Where do you fall short of goodness? Write a short prayer, asking Him to help point out these areas to you. Then ask Him to help you work to eliminate those sins from your life.

_____

_____

_____

_____

Goodness is more than just having good morals and avoiding sin; it's sharing God's goodness with the people around us. It's taking our focus off of ourselves and looking for ways to help others.

Are you generous? Are you doing what you can to benefit others instead of focusing on yourself? How can you share God's goodness with someone in your path today? Write a short prayer, asking God to help you take the focus off yourself and onto the needs of the people around you. Ask Him to help you share His goodness with others.

_____

_____

_____

_____

Read Galatians 6:10 and write it here:

_____

_____

_____

_____

Remember this verse as you go throughout your day, and ask God to give you opportunities to do good to all people.

Day Nine:
The Seventh Fruit of the Spirit

In your own words, what does it mean to be "faithful" in a relationship?

_____

_____

_____

_____

Most people think of it in terms of a romantic relationship, but you can (and should) be faithful in any and every type of relationship you have. Being faithful means being loyal. It means standing by the person and being someone who can be counted on.

When it comes to your relationship with God, it means you trust Him and believe in His promises. We live in a world that often says, "I'll believe it when I see it." A world that doubts everything. But being faithful means we can say, "God, I know I don't see it yet, but I believe in You and I know You are going to come through." It can be a real challenge, even for long-time believers.

Being faithful to God also means you're making a regular effort to be in contact with Him. I know that sounds strange – it's not like you can send Him a text or call Him up, right? But you CAN hear from Him every day, through reading His Word. And you CAN talk to Him every day – all day, if you want to – by just praying. Sharing your life with Him. Asking Him for advice.

So ask yourself this: are you faithful to God? Are you trusting Him, believing in Him, making a daily effort to talk to Him and read the Bible? Talk to God about this. If there are areas where you can improve in this, ask God to help you. Write a short prayer to Him, asking Him to help you be a faithful follower of His.

_____

_____

_____

_____

Remember that being faithful applies to all of our relationships – not just our relationships with God. It means being loyal to your friends, being there for them and standing by their sides. It means being dedicated to your boyfriends or girlfriends (current or future) by treating them the way God would have you treat them. It means being reliable for your family, loving them and showing up for them.

Write one more short prayer to God, asking Him to help you be a faithful in all your relationships, both present and future.

_____

_____

_____

_____

Day Ten:
The Eighth Fruit of the Spirit

This next fruit gets a bad rap, but it's undeserved. It's something that many in today's world see as a weakness…when in reality, it takes a strength that most don't have.

So what is this fruit? It's "gentleness."

Gentle people are soft and calm. They're helpful. They look for the best in others, even when it isn't easy to see. They don't see themselves as "better" than anyone else. They don't lash out with anger, but offer forgiveness whenever they can.

In the world we live in, gentleness isn't valued. But don't mistake it to be a character flaw. Jesus, who was strong enough not just to endure the cross but defeat death by rising from the grave, was a prime example of what it means to be gentle.

In John chapter 8, the religious leaders brought a woman to Jesus. They had caught her in sin red-handed and stood her out in front of everyone, ready to stone her. But Jesus refused to join the religious leaders in their "high and mighty" crusade against this sinner. Instead of turning His nose up at her, He stooped down to the ground and wrote in the dirt. Then He straightened up, turned to the people, and challenged them by inviting anyone who was perfect to throw the first stone at this woman.

One by one, the people walked away, until only Jesus and the woman were left. He didn't yell at her. He didn't belittle her or tell her what a horrible person she was. Instead, Jesus told her gently to go and turn away from her sin.

Are you humble? Forgiving? Are you able to look at others with love, seeing them the way God sees them instead of the way the world does? Have an honest conversation with God about this. Write a short prayer, asking Him to help you see how you could be gentler in your interactions with others.

_____

_____

_____

The Bible has many, many verses about the importance of having "gentleness" as a character trait. One of those verses is Ephesians 4:2. Read this verse and write it here:

_____

_____

_____

_____

Work on committing this verse to memory this week.

Day Eleven:
The Ninth Fruit of the Spirit

Before we study the final fruit on the list, let's start today by giving thanks to God for someone or something He has blessed you with.

_____

_____

_____

_____

The last fruit listed in Galatians is something called self-control. Self-control is about disciplining yourself and avoiding situations that will lead you into sin. This will look different for all of us, because we all struggle with different sins. It's setting boundaries and keeping your words and actions in check.

For example, let's say you struggle with gossip. It's likely when you find yourself around certain friends, you will end up gossiping about someone. So how do you steer clear of these situations? Well, one obvious solution is to spend less time with those friends, though that isn't always possible or even something you *want* to do. Another option is to approach the friend gently and just be honest. Say up front, "I'm really trying to stop talking bad about people. Can you help me with that goal?"

Maybe gossiping isn't an issue for you, but you struggle with addiction issues. You have to make it a point to avoid any situation that puts those substances in front of you. It won't be easy. It will mean saying no to party invites, hanging out with certain people, or whatever it may be. But having self-control means you're able to recognize those tempting circumstances and stay away from them.

Are you able to walk away from temptation? Do you steer clear of situations that will cause you to sin? Ask God to help you with this. He knows it isn't easy, especially when so many around you don't have (or care about) that kind of self-control. Write a short prayer, getting as specific as you can in asking God for help with the areas where you struggle.

_____

_____

_____

_____

When it gets tough, remember this: God didn't give us rules or guidelines to be the "mean" parent who keeps us from having any fun. He loves us more than we could ever understand, and He only wants what is best for us. God can see the results of sin. He knows the way that gossip is going to tear someone down. He knows those addictions are going to harm your body, your mind, and likely other people as well. He wants to keep us safe. He wants a life for you that's filled with joy and peace, and He knows sin will keep you from it.

When temptations seem to be stronger than you are, read 1 Corinthians 10:13. Write it here:

_____

_____

_____

_____

Remember: God is bigger than any temptation, and with His help, you can rise above anything this world throws at you.

Day Twelve:
One Last Look at the Fruits of the Spirit

We've spent a lot of time breaking down the "fruits" that Christians should be producing in their lives every day, because it's an important list to get us started as we become the *new creation* God is molding us to be. Let's take a look at the full list of fruits one more time before we move on to something new.

Read Galatians 5:22-23, and write it here once again:

_____

_____

_____

_____

*Memorization tip: Write the verse on a post-it note and place it somewhere you will see it often, like on your bedroom mirror or inside your locker. Read it repeatedly to help it start sticking in your mind. This is a great verse to know and keep in your heart!

As a Christian, these are the fruits that should be coming from us. If they're not, who's going to call us Christians?

First of all, don't beat yourself up if you don't feel like you're doing a good job of showing all of them yet. You don't become a Christian and automatically produce every single one of those fruits. There were probably some on that list you feel "better" at than others, right? That's okay. That's where you need to ask the Holy Spirit to help you. For example, do you struggle with patience? Ask God to help you become more patient. The beautiful thing is, all those fruits mentioned are for *all* Christians. So, even if you don't feel like you're a very patient person, you're not meant to stay that way. You're a work in progress.

When you became a Christian, God began working inside of you. Read

Philippians 1:6 and write it here:

_____

_____

_____

_____

Remember that when God starts something, He finishes it. He will bring it to completion – He won't leave you flailing out there. He will keep working in you, molding you to be a little more like Jesus every day.

Study that list of the fruit of the Spirit, and take an honest look inside yourself. Which fruits do you most struggle with? Write a short prayer to God, confessing your struggles. Ask God to help you start producing and exhibiting those qualities more and more every day. Ask Him to work in your heart to mold you into the person you're meant to be.

_____

_____

_____

_____

Day Thirteen:
Jesus is the Vine

Many fruits, like grapes, depend on a vine to grow. They may grow out from the vine, but they have to remain connected to it. They depend on the vine for life and growth. Without it, they will only last for a little while before they are worthless and withered.

Jesus compared our relationship with Him to a vine and branches. Read John 15:5 and write it here:

_____

_____

_____

_____

Jesus is the vine we have to depend on. Without Him, there is no life. When we are connected to Him – truly connected, walking closely with Him – we will bear that fruit we've spent the last several days breaking down. That fruit can only come from Him. Abiding in Him means we live our lives with Him, realizing that if we disconnect from that vine, we are powerless. Lifeless. Without Him, we are like those branches that are ripped away from the plant, only to wither up and waste away. When we disconnect from Him, we have no hope for the future.

There are a lot of people who claim to be Christians, but don't truly know Jesus. Read John 8:31-32 and write those verses here:

_____

_____

_____

_____

These are the words of Jesus. So who did He call His true disciples?

Those who abide in His Word. Those who live their lives, seeking His truth with every step they take. It's more than showing up at church for an hour or two on Sunday. It's more than praying a quick prayer every now and then. It's digging in to your Bible. It's pressing in to Jesus – learning about Him, talking to Him, imitating Him.

Write a short prayer to God, asking Him to help you live the life He has intended for you by seeking Jesus and remaining in Him every single day. Ask Him to help you depend on Him completely, knowing that without Him, you are worthless. Ask Him to help you stay connected to Him so you can grow and thrive and produce the Fruit of the Spirit.

_____

_____

_____

_____

Day Fourteen:
It's All About Relationship with God

Many people have this idea about God in their heads. They picture Him as this old guy up in the sky who watches them and waits for them to mess up. But nothing could be further from the truth. Our God is loving. He is good. And what He wants more than anything is to have a real relationship with you. A big part of becoming a new creation is forming that bond with Him.

Through prayer, we have a direct line of communication with God. That line is open twenty-four hours a day, seven days a week. You get to choose how often you use it. He is always waiting and ready to listen. He actually wants you to share your life with Him – your struggles, your worries, your failures and successes. He wants you to talk to Him, asking Him for what you need and thanking Him for what He has given you.

A lot of people think of praying as just another item on their to-do list. But good prayer – the kind God intends for us to experience – is so much more than just talking at some invisible being in the sky we can't see or hear. Good prayer is about a relationship with a real, living God who listens and even talks back.

The first step to experiencing that good prayer is to find a private place and get alone – just you and God. Jesus modeled this over and over again during His time in this world. Read Mark 1:35 and write it here:

_____

_____

_____

_____

Jesus had stayed up really late the night before, healing person after person who came to see Him. But the next morning, instead of sleeping in, He got up before the sun even rose. He got away from His friends and the crowds of people who flocked to Him so He could spend time alone with God.

Jesus knew how important it was to have a conversation with His Father. More important than sleep. It was the first thing He did before He faced the world and began His day. He got away from the noise. He didn't let anyone or anything distract Him so He could focus solely on praying.

If Jesus did this, shouldn't we?

To start getting more from your prayer life with God, first ask yourself this: where can you go to be alone with God? Think about it. Do you have a private place where you won't be bothered by others? Some close themselves in bedrooms or even closets. Others like to get out of the house and take a solo walk somewhere quiet. It doesn't have to be hours – you can start with ten or fifteen minutes.

Make a plan and write it down. Where will you go? When will you try to carve that time into your schedule? Try to create a habit you can stick to.

_____

_____

_____

Be honest – what distracts you when you're trying to pray? Is it your friends? Your cell phone? Video games? You have to be intentional about having that conversation with God and get in a space where it's just you and Him. Think about this: if a friend came to hang out with you, but he kept getting sidetracked because of texts, social media, or looking around at what else was going on, neither one of you would get much out of your conversation, would you? God deserves your undivided attention – remember, you have His. So what distractions do you need to leave behind when you go to spend your quiet time with God?

_____

_____

_____

_____

Day Fifteen:
How to Pray – the Jesus Way

Okay, so you found your quiet spot. No distractions around you; it's just you and God. You bow your head and close your eyes and open your mouth to talk to Him…but you have no idea what to say or where to start. Has this ever happened to you? You just aren't sure what to pray about, or you can't find the words to say?

A lot of people think they have to pray these "perfect" prayers in order for God to listen, but that's not true. The Pharisees – the religious leaders during Jesus's time – tried to impress people by praying these long, fancy prayers out loud so everyone would know how religious they were. But Jesus said that's not what God wants from you. He gave a model prayer – something simple – that God's people could use when it's time to talk to their Father.

While this prayer was short and sweet, it packed a lot of important stuff in there. Over the next few days, we're going to break it down, looking at each part of it to see why it's important and how it fits in your life today.

Let's start at the beginning of His prayer instructions. Read Matthew 6:9 and write it here:

_____

_____

_____

_____

Notice what He did in the very first line. Before He ever asked for anything or talked about Himself at all, He gave God the credit for being who He is – our Father in heaven. He also said that God's name was *hallowed*, which is a fancy way of saying He is highly honored.

It's so important to start our prayers off by giving God the glory He deserves, recognizing Him as our Father. When we can't see Him, it's easy to forget who He really is. Sometimes we tend to imagine Him as this genie in the sky who just sits up there, waiting to grant our wishes. But in reality, it's not about us. It's about Him – the One who made us and gave us everything we have.

It's difficult to truly picture God, because what God looks like is beyond our ability to understand or describe. Go check out the book of Revelation if you want an idea. It was written by John, one of the disciples, who received visions from God. Revelation 1 describes His face shining like the sun and His eyes like fire. Revelation 4 has this amazing picture of God sitting on His throne, surrounded by an emerald-like rainbow with flashes of lightning and peals of thunder that came out of it.

If you ever find yourself forgetting how *big* God truly is – how majestic and amazing and incredible – try to picture those images from Revelation 1 and 4. It's bigger than our brains can really comprehend. But that's the point: God is so much more than we can ever truly grasp in our small human minds. When we remember that, we keep Him in the right perspective.

He doesn't exist to serve us. WE exist to serve HIM. We are nothing compared to who He is…and yet, for some reason we'll never really understand, He loves us more than we can ever know.

When you come to God in your prayer time, start by recognizing God for who He really is. Picture Him sitting on that throne, surrounded by angels and rainbows and thunder and lightning. If you were in the room with Him, what would be your response? You would likely fall to your knees in awe and respect. Approach your prayer time that way this morning. Before you ask Him for anything, give Him the glory and honor He deserves. How can you do that, in your own words? Try it here.

_____

_____

_____

_____

Day Sixteen:
How to Pray – the Jesus Way, Part Two

You're picturing God in heaven, sitting on His throne. You've recognized Him as your Father, and you've given Him the honor and glory He really deserves.

Now what? Do you just jump right in and start asking for your needs or wants? According to the model Jesus gave us, there's something else we need to do first.

Read Matthew 6:10 and write it here:

_____

_____

_____

Notice something about those words? The "Your" (or "Thy" in some translations) He was talking to was God. Right away, He said He wanted God's kingdom, God's will, in His life. Not His own will. God's will. He wanted God's purpose, God's plan. Not His own ideas of what that should look like.

I know we like to think we know what's best for our lives. We talk to God about our own plans for our lives and ask Him to help them happen, our way.

Don't get me wrong: *that's okay*. It's okay to share your heart with God. It's okay to ask for things you need or even just want. He already knows what's on your mind – no reason to try to hide it from Him. Put it out there. Lay out your dreams and plans for Him.

BUT….you also need to recognize that He knows what's best for you. He created you. He already knows exactly how your life is going to play out. Of course He knows what you need, and He knows how to best meet those needs. Your job is to trust Him and pray that HIS will is done in your life… not your own.

On the last night Jesus was here in this world, He went away to pray. He knew this was the night He would be arrested and put on trial. The cross was coming, along with all the pain and humiliation it would bring. He was overcome with deep sadness.

He fell on His face and started praying. Read His prayer in Matthew 26:39 and write it here:

_____

_____

_____

_____

He dreaded what was coming. He knew it would be an agonizing, painful death, but above that, He knew He would bear the sin of the whole world while He hung on that cross. Yet as much as He dreaded it, He knew it as God's perfect will. He made a decision to fulfill what God had planned.

Jesus got it. He knew that, as difficult as the coming hours would be, it was part of a bigger plan – something amazing God was going to do. He knew that His sacrifice on that cross would make a way for you to be in Heaven someday. And so, above everything else, He wanted to do God's will. Because He realized that God's plan will always be better than anything else.

There may be difficult things you're going through. There may be things you desperately want to happen in your life, things you're begging God to do or give you.

But this is the part where your faith comes in: You have to be willing to put His will above your own. When you can say to God, "Above everything else, I want what *You* want for my life," that's when He can really begin to make incredible things happen. Write a short prayer here, asking God for His will in your life above your own in your own words.

_____

_____

Day Seventeen:
How to Pray – the Jesus Way, Part Three

From the time you're in preschool, you begin planning for your future. You dream of becoming a cop, or a ballerina, or a professional baseball player, or a princess. As you grow, your dreams take a more serious turn. Adults counsel you to try hard in school, because your grades will matter for your future. You start hearing about colleges and scholarships and careers.

And all that stuff is so important. You have to prepare for your future and make decisions that will shape the direction your life will take. In no way should that stuff be ignored or lessened.

But don't let yourself get so sucked in to your future that you try to live there in your mind. No matter your goals, you will only get there one day at a time. Focus on today, the here and now. Live in this moment.

Read the next part of the model prayer, Matthew 6:11, and write it here:

_____

_____

_____

As humans, we have things we need each day. There are physical needs, like food or healing from sickness. But there are emotional and spiritual needs, too, like strength for a difficult task or help with a major problem. On any given day, we all have different needs and struggles in our lives. Whatever your need is, God wants you to bring it to Him and trust Him to provide for you.

Notice how simple Jesus kept it: He asked for bread for today. He didn't ask for unlimited bread. He didn't ask for unlimited money, either, to buy big, fancy meals every day. He asked for what He needed right then to get through the day.

Have you ever read about Moses and the Israelites in the wilderness back in the Old Testament? As they journeyed from Egypt to the Promised Land, they found themselves without food. To solve this problem, God literally rained food down on them from heaven and gave them instructions to gather enough for each day. Only on the day before the Sabbath were they to gather two days' worth of it.

Being typical humans, some of them got greedy. They tried to gather two days' amount, even when they weren't supposed to. Do you know what happened to the extra? It grew moldy and stinky and full of worms. God was teaching them to trust Him to provide every single day, just as He promised He would. He will give you what you need, too.

Our God loves you, and He knows even your smallest needs. Think for a moment of how much He has given you that you never even asked Him for. It's a huge list, isn't it? He wants you to trust Him with those needs, to bring them to Him each day and know that He will provide. So what do you need today? Use the space below to write a short prayer to God, turning your needs over to Him. Remember, no need is too big or too small to talk to God about. Give it all to Him and be ready to see how He works in you and for you.

_____

_____

_____

_____

Day Eighteen:
How to Pray – the Jesus Way, Part Four

God knows we all have needs. We have illnesses and weaknesses. We have problems and difficult situations. We all need help in different ways, and we can bring all of that to the feet of Jesus and trust that He can take care of our individual needs.

But the one thing we all have in common is this: *we all need forgiveness*.

Sin is the thing that separates you from God. More than anything else – even more than those important needs like food, water, clothing, and shelter – we need forgiveness of sin.

Thankfully, God is always willing to offer His forgiveness. It's why He sent Jesus here to take our place on that cross, so that He could conquer death once and for all. And once we accept His gift of Jesus, receiving God's forgiveness is as simple as asking for it.

The moment you ask God to, He not only forgives your sin, He wipes your slate clean. He doesn't hold your past against you.

But it's not a one-and-done thing. When you ask Jesus to be your Lord and Savior, admitting to God that you are a sinner and need His forgiveness, it doesn't automatically mean you'll never sin again. The devil doesn't give up that easily. Temptation is all around you, and sin is a daily battle. It will be the rest of your life, unfortunately.

Asking forgiveness has to become a regular part of our prayer life. Read Matthew 6:12 and write it here:

_____

_____

_____

_____

Side note: Jesus never sinned. He is the only One who ever walked this earth and lived a perfect life. But He included this line in His model prayer because He knew without a doubt that we could never be perfect. Sin is part of this broken world, and it's something we all must deal with.

When you mess up, and you will, just admit it to God and ask Him to help you do better. And guess what? There will be times when you sin without even realizing it. You will never have a day when you are "perfect," because you're a human, and it's just not possible. Ask God to forgive you for those sins you commit by accident as well.

Okay, here's the harder part: we have to pay attention to the second part of that line, too. Because if God is going to keep forgiving us over and over, giving us chance after chance that we don't deserve, He expects us to offer forgiveness to others as well.

That's really difficult to do sometimes, isn't it? Because people will hurt you and let you down. They may apologize, and they may not – either way, God says it isn't up to us to decide if they deserve forgiveness. He doesn't want us to hold grudges and cling to anger, reliving the things that have caused us pain. He wants us to let it all go, through forgiveness.

To be clear, *forgiveness* doesn't mean pretending the pain didn't happen. If someone is hurting you, physically or mentally, you are allowed to forgive from a distance and protect yourself. You don't have to stay in the situation, but you *do* have to let go of the anger and ill feelings you have toward the person.

Here's the deal: holding on to anger and pain doesn't hurt the person who caused it. It hurts *you*. It causes stress. Depression. Anxiety. It can even lead to heart problems and other health issues. When God tells you to forgive others, it's as much for your own sake as it is for the other person.

So how do you do it? How do you let go of the anger and pain? You probably won't be able to do it alone. You have to take it to God and ask for His help. You need Him to help you release all those negative feelings and find some sort of peace with the situation.

Write a short prayer to God, talking to Him about forgiveness. Confess the sins you've been struggling with lately, asking His forgiveness and His help avoiding those temptations from here on out. Also, ask Him to help you deal with any anger and pain you're holding onto in your heart. Ask Him to help you forgive, just as He forgives you.

_____

_____

_____

_____

Day Nineteen:
How to Pray – the Jesus Way, Part Five

When you see Satan depicted in the media, he's usually this little guy wearing all red carrying a pitchfork. But the truth is, he won't appear to you like that. You would *know* to avoid that little red guy. In reality, Satan is the master of disguise. When he approaches you, he will look like what you think you want. That's the thing about sin – it definitely looks appealing. If it didn't, it wouldn't be temptation, would it?

The moment you decided to follow Jesus, Satan became your enemy. His goal is to distract you and set you back in your walk with God. He does whatever he can to keep God's kingdom from accomplishing anything on earth.

His tactics have basically been the same since the beginning of time. Back in the Adam and Eve days, he started pulling out his tricks. He got Eve to focus on the ONE thing God told her not to do, taking her attention from all the good things God had given her that surrounded her. He got her to question what God actually said and led her to disobey the only rule she had been given.

This is the same method he uses today. He wants you to stop focusing on all the blessings God has given you and focus on the ground rules God has given. But the thing is, life as a Christian was never meant to be boring, though Satan loves to try to make you believe that. God knows some of those things the world has to offer may make you think you're happy for a little while, but will ultimately lead to your destruction.

And that's the thing: Satan loves destruction. He makes it his mission to make that sin look appealing, knowing it will lead to nothing good and only pull you away from God's purpose for your life. He has planted the lie in our society that you should "follow your heart," when he knows the heart is deceptive. He knows our emotions are unsteady and change all the time. He knows those sinful desires will only lead to trouble when they're followed.

That's why when Jesus finished off His prayer, He asked God for protection from it all. Read Matthew 6:13 and write it here:

_____

_____

_____

_____

Jesus knew how easy it is to fall victim to temptation. He knew Satan would be looking for every opportunity to attack.

So how do you recognize Satan when he comes at you? You have to be alert and watching. You have to recognize sin for what it is. You have to know God's Word and believe what it says. You have to be willing to believe it over your own heart at times, which isn't easy when emotions can feel so strong and so right.

On Jesus's last night here on earth, He went out to pray. His disciples were supposed to be keeping watch, supporting Him, but they kept falling asleep. Jesus warned them to be watching and praying, staying alert at all times. He knew how easy it can be to become distracted by the world and even physical needs, like sleep, but he also knew the difficult situation they were all about to go through.

Like the disciples, we also must be watching and praying. Our world today is full of distractions, and when we take our eyes off Jesus, it is so easy to get caught up in other things. We have to ask God to help us avoid the temptations that stand in our path so we can stay on course.

Remember this: Satan may be strong and he may be smart, but he is not God's equal. With God's help, there is nothing you will face that you can't defeat. Write a short prayer to God, asking Him to help you avoid the temptations that come your way. If you have specific sins or temptations you're struggling with right now, turn them over to God and ask Him to give you the strength it takes to walk away from it.

_____

_____

_____

_____
_____
_____
_____
_____
_____

Day Twenty: True Belief

Let's talk about the idea of true belief. We will look at John 3:16, one of the most famous verses in the Bible. Read it and write it here:

_____

_____

_____

_____

Jesus spoke this verse in the middle of that conversation He had with Nicodemus, the one we talked about in an earlier devotion. It's a beautiful promise: if we believe in Jesus, we will live in heaven someday. If we believe He is the Son of God and that He gave His life on the cross for us, we have an amazing eternity in store for us.

So what does it mean to believe? It goes beyond simply admitting Jesus is real. Even Satan and the demons believe Jesus is the Son of God. True belief is more than believing something in your head. It's about *action*. It's about hearing the words Jesus spoke, and putting them into practice.

Someone once compared it to a house fire. If you *know* the house is on fire, you're going to act, right? You wouldn't just sit there at the kitchen table and say to yourself, "Yes, I believe the house is on fire, but I'm not going to do anything about it." You would jump into action, right? It's the same concept as beginning to follow Jesus. When you become a Christian, you can't just sit back and keep living life the same way you always have. It's more than just saying a prayer and asking Jesus into your heart. It's a daily walk, a daily effort to leave your sins behind and become the person God made you to be.

Jesus gave instructions for those who want to follow Him. Read Luke 9:23 and write it here:

_____

_____

_____

_____

Take up a cross? What does that mean? When you imagine carrying a cross, which weighs up to 300 pounds, you know the pain and suffering it must cause. Mentally, we have to take up that cross each day, knowing it's going to take effort to deny our own desires and temptations that come our way. As soon as a sinful thought enters – a temptation to lie, or gossip, or whatever it may be – you choose to deny it. You choose to reject the idea, not letting it get past your mind and into your heart.

It won't be easy, and at times it will feel painful. Choosing to deny yourself the temptation of going along with others when they sin is difficult when we are born with the desire to fit in and be accepted. But taking up that cross leads to transformation. When you deny yourself and the sinful urges you have, God can work in you and create the best version of yourself.

Are you ready to do that? Are you ready to deny yourself and carry the cross of Jesus every day? Write a short prayer here, talking to God about it. Ask Him to show you what it will look like in your life to put your belief into action. He knows it won't be easy for you, so ask Him for His help. When you're ready to follow Him, He has an amazing journey prepared for you!

_____

_____

_____

_____

Day Twenty-One: Be Thankful

Imagine you woke up this morning, and you only had the people and things you thanked God for yesterday. Who would still be here? What would you still have?

As humans, we often get it backwards – we focus on what we *don't* have instead of the things we have. We believe when we get what we want, *then* we will feel happy. But God says it's just the opposite. It's when we come to Him with a heart that is thankful for what we have that we experience His joy and peace.

Read 1 Thessalonians 5:18 and write it here:

_____

_____

_____

_____

People have done studies on gratitude and its effects. People who regularly list the things they are thankful for have a more positive outlook on life. They are less likely to be jealous and self-centered, and they have higher self-esteem. Feeling grateful actually improves sleep, mood, and immunity to sickness. It also decreases depression, anxiety, and pain and improves relationships.

If this was a medicine, we would all be taking it! It's no wonder God tells us to give thanks in all circumstances.

A grateful heart works like a magnet. The more you look for blessings, the more reasons for gratitude your heart will collect. If I told you to look around the room for anything you could find that's red, you would likely spot many items. But after doing so, if I told you to list everything you found that was blue, you wouldn't be able to list as many. Why? *That's not what you were looking for.* You were looking for red items, so that's what your brain noted. It works the same way in life: if you look for reasons to be thankful, you will find them. But if you look for things to complain about, trust me, you'll find lots of those, too. You have to make it a point to tell your brain what to look for.

Read Psalm 100:4-5. Write it here:

_____

_____

_____

_____

When you come to God in prayer today, don't start with your list of needs and requests. Start by thanking Him for His many, many blessings. Not only does it bless God and lift Him up, it will help you as well. It will help you experience His joy and bring you closer to Him. It will help you get through the hard stuff that life throws your way.

Write a short prayer to God, thanking Him for what He has given you. No matter what is going on in your life, you can always find reasons to praise Him. Ask Him to help you keep your focus on gratitude today and look for those blessings He puts in your path.

_____

_____

_____

_____

Day Twenty-Two:
Jesus > the World

How many times have you looked out at the world and wished for just one thing to change in your life? *If I were smarter, I'd be happy. If I were thinner, I would feel good about myself. If I were more popular...If I had a boyfriend/girlfriend...If I had more money...If I had a different home life... If I could move away from here...* Whatever the thing is that we wish for, we trick ourselves into believing it's the one thing that would give us happiness. With it, we would finally find contentment.

It's human nature to focus on those things we don't have and convince ourselves those things are the key to finding fulfillment. But what you have in Jesus is greater than anything you don't have. You have a God who loves you unconditionally. A God who is working for you and protecting you. A God who sent His Son to die on the cross for you so you have a perfect eternity in store for you. In Jesus, you have everything!

Philippians 4:13 is one of the most famous verses in the Bible. Read it and write it here:

_____

_____

_____

_____

This verse is empowering. No wonder it's a famous verse. But so many people who quote it miss the meaning and context in which it was written. Did you know the Apostle Paul wrote this verse from prison? When you look at the verse before it, you get a clearer picture of what Paul actually meant when he said it. Read Philippians 4:12 and write it here:

_____

_____

In every circumstance, Paul had learned the secret of being content. It didn't come from anything he could find in this world – it came only from Jesus. Even in prison, he found contentment in Jesus!

There's nothing the world has to offer that can completely fulfill you. Not family, not friends, not your boyfriend or girlfriend, not followers, not sports, not video games, not music, not money, not success. Sure, those things can be wonderful things, but they won't fill the emptiness in your soul that was designed for relationship with your Creator. Only Jesus can do that.

Are you finding your fulfillment in Jesus today? Write a short prayer, asking God to help you. Ask Him to help you remember His strength can shine in you, even in the areas where you fall short. Ask Him to help you keep your focus on Him above everything else, finding the contentment only He can give.

Day Twenty-Three: Washing Feet

When Jesus's time on earth was almost up, He did something truly amazing. He was about to give His life on the cross. Judas was already scheming to betray Him and give Him over to the ones who would put Him to death. He knew His time was almost up. But in that time before His final moments, He rose from the table where His disciples sat, poured water into a basin, and began to wash the dirty feet of His disciples.

Sounds weird, I know. But in Bible times, this was very common. People traveled on dirt roads wearing sandals – their feet got dirty. This job of washing guests' feet usually went to a lowly servant, not the King of kings! The disciples were shocked. Some even tried to refuse, but Jesus insisted. He humbled Himself to do this job, serving His disciples even in this task that many found disgusting and demeaning.

Jesus knows we can't "wash" away our own sin and flaws. Only He can do that. He wants us to bring our mess to Him and let Him do what only He can do. But He also washed the feet of His disciples as an example for us.

It's a very different concept than what the world teaches. *Build a name for yourself,* they say. *Work hard, get to the top, and step on anyone in your way in order to get there.* Success, in the world's eyes, involves riches and fancy things. Lots of important friends.

But Jesus had a different idea. Read Mark 10:43-45 and write it here:

_____

_____

_____

_____

Jesus may have been the King of kings, but He didn't live that way. He lived a humble life and spent His time with people society deemed unworthy.

He gave His time and energy to help the poor, the sick, and the hurting. He didn't put value on *things*.

When He washed the feet of His disciples that evening, He became a model for us. Read John 13:14 and write it here:

_____
_____
_____
_____

If Jesus Christ Himself can wash the filthy, dirt-caked feet of His followers, is there really any task that is "beneath" us?

So ask yourself this: where can you serve others today? Where can you follow the example of Jesus and show love through your actions for others? How can you humble yourself and reach out to someone? Write a short prayer to God, asking Him to put opportunities in your path to serve those in need. Ask Him to help you be humble like Jesus, loving and giving of your time and energy to help someone today.

_____
_____
_____
_____
_____
_____

Day Twenty-Four: Bold Faith

What is faith? Faith is so much more than just believing in God. It's more than believing He sent Jesus to die on the cross for your sins. Real faith is trusting God to lead you – no matter where that may be.

You can be sure that there will be times that God will lead you out of your comfort zone. The Bible is full of stories where He did just that. Noah built an ark when God told him it would flood – though he had never seen rain before. Abraham packed up his belongings and his family and left his home to move to a strange land, trusting God to make him a father of many nations – though he was an old man and had no children. Moses stood up to Pharaoh and led God's people out of slavery – though he had a speech impediment.

When you follow God, you may have to take some risks. You may feel God pulling you to do something you don't feel comfortable doing. You may doubt yourself. You may feel terrified of what others will do or say if you act on God's calling.

Read 2 Timothy 1:7. Write it here:

_____

_____

_____

_____

One thing to remember is that fear is not from God. You have to push it (and pray it) out of your mind. You can take comfort knowing that if God leads you to do something, He will be your help. Sometimes it takes a change of mindset: God's calling isn't always about protecting yourself from all suffering and discomfort. It's about trusting and following, knowing that in the midst of whatever you face, God is there. He will never leave you to face the world on your own.

Joshua 1:9 offers some advice and comfort for facing life with bold faith. Read it and write it here:

_____

_____

_____

_____

You don't need to see what's ahead to trust Him...*just walk.*

God is still using people with bold faith today. Those Bible heroes weren't perfect. They didn't always follow God's directing the way they were supposed to. But they weren't afraid to act in faith, even when they didn't know exactly where God's calling would lead them. And because of that, God used them to do amazing things.

Talk to God about this. Write a short prayer to God, asking Him to help you recognize His voice when He speaks into your mind and heart. Ask Him to help you follow His calling with boldness so you can make an impact for His kingdom.

_____

_____

_____

_____

Day Twenty-Five: Feeding Your Mind

When you throw a sponge into a bucket of water, what happens? The sponge absorbs the water, soaking up as much as it possibly can until you lift it out of the water and the water overflows from it. As you carry the sponge away from the bucket, water drips from the sponge onto everything in its path.

Your mind works like that sponge. All day long, information is thrown at it and absorbed, whether you realize it or not. What you hear at school. What you watch on TV or your phone. What music you listen to. It's all soaking in, shaping your thoughts. And when you walk away, whatever you absorb is what comes pouring out in your words and actions. It truly shapes who you become.

So what "bucket" are you choosing for your mind? I promise you, most of what the world has to offer as far as soaking your mind is not in line with God's love and purpose. In fact, the majority of it goes directly against God's Word.

You have to counteract it. You have to make it a point to let your mind "soak" in the Word of God. You have to make that quiet time to spend talking to God and reading your Bible.

There's an old saying: "Garbage in, garbage out." If you allow your brain to soak up what the world has to offer, it's what your thoughts will crank out as well. It's that simple: if you spend most of your time reading, watching, and listening to worldly things, you're going to look and sound just like the world does. And as a child of God, that's not who you're called to be.

Read 2 Corinthians 6:17 and write it here:

_____

_____

_____

It's a call to be separate. Set apart. You were never meant to look and act like everyone else. You are unique, a masterpiece of God. You weren't made to be one of the crowd. You are a child of God, and were made in His image. People so often feel this need to fit in, which makes this call difficult at times. But it's always worth it.

So how do you counteract it? You can't always completely control what you hear and see. But you can control what you *choose* to feed your mind. You can choose the shows and videos you watch. You can choose the music you listen to. You can choose how you spend your free time.

Read Matthew 4:4 and write it here:

_____

_____

_____

_____

Jesus compares God's Word to bread, or food. We eat food every day, right? We *need* it to live. Think of the Bible as something you need, too: you need it to live and thrive. Treat it like food. You truly do need it regularly. Do you eat only on Sundays? Of course not. Hearing the Bible at church for an hour, one day a week, won't cut it, either. You need the Word of God *daily* to overpower the garbage. When you're forced to soak in what the world has to offer every day, the only way to even attempt to counteract it is to feed on what God says.

Opening the Bible and trying to read it on your own can be a daunting task. Today, ask God to help you open its pages and focus on what He has for you in it. Ask Him to help you overcome any obstacles so you can focus on the text and truly let your mind absorb what he has to tell you. Write a short prayer, asking God to help you choose wisely what you feed your mind today. Ask Him to help you eliminate the garbage and be set apart as He has called you to be.

Day Twenty-Six:
The Power of Words

Have you ever been hurt by something someone said to you? Sometimes words can do more damage than weapons. Comments from others can stick with you, shaping the way you feel about yourself. Unfortunately, it's basically impossible to live life without being deeply hurt by someone's words at some point. Words have enormous power. In the Bible, James compares our words to a spark that can ignite an entire forest fire.

Most people speak thousands of words every single day. But how often do we really think about our words before we speak? Jesus had a warning for us in Matthew 12:36-37. Read it and write the verses here:

_____

_____

_____

Imagine facing God someday, answering for every hateful or rude word you said. Scary thought! When you consider the fact that God is listening to what we say to others, you realize you should choose your words wisely.

Read Proverbs 18:21 and write it here:

_____

_____

_____

_____

Death and life – that's a lot of power. Your words have the ability to build someone up or tear someone down. That's a lot of pressure to think before you speak, isn't it?

So how *should* we speak, as Christians? Read Colossians 3:8 and write it here:

_____

_____

_____

_____

Have you ever lashed out at someone when you're mad, even regretting the things you said later? Have you ever gossiped about someone, spreading rumors and sharing hurtful information? Have you ever said something inappropriate? You probably hear a lot of that kind of talk every day, and it's hard to shut that stuff out. And if we're being honest, for whatever reason, it's hard for us not to repeat that joke or the newest gossip. When you're surrounded by the kind of talk the Bible warns us to avoid every single day, it's difficult to remember to watch your own words.

So how do you do it? Well, it comes back to the idea of feeding your mind. You can't totally avoid hearing that kind of talk, but you can control how much of it you take it. You have the power to decide who you surround yourself with. You can decide what music you listen to and what you watch. If you're absorbing inappropriate or hateful talk all the time, of course that's what's going to come out of your own mouth. Steer clear of it. Even when it's not easy. Even when you feel left out.

Before you speak to someone, ask yourself this: are my words kind? Are they going to encourage this person? To build him or her up somehow? Here's a test you can use to decide if your words are acceptable: if Jesus was standing next to you right now, would you feel comfortable enough to say them? If the answer is *no*, those words aren't worth saying.

Write a short prayer to God, asking for His help with this. Watching your words is one of the most challenging parts of being a Christian. That's why it's so important to pray about it. With God's help, you can get better every day, learning to choose your words wisely.

Day Twenty-Seven: Handling Temptation

You know that Jesus led a perfect life here on earth. But did you know that even He was tempted? Right after He was baptized, Satan swooped in. (The timing is not a coincidence, by the way. If you find temptation all around you right after you give your life to Jesus, don't be surprised – it's Satan's method.) He waited until Jesus had fasted forty days and nights – so you can imagine how hungry He was – and then made a move. He tried to get Jesus to turn the stones into bread. Jesus could have done it easily, but He didn't. Instead, He came back with a Bible verse about how man doesn't live on bread alone, but by God's words. He trusted God to provide what He needed.

Satan came at him again. He took Jesus up high and tried to get him to throw Himself down, reasoning that if Jesus was really the Son of God, angels would come to save Him. He even cited a quote from Psalms to back up his claim – because yes, the devil knows Bible verses, too. Again, Jesus came back with Scripture, reminding Satan that the Bible says not to tempt or test God. He chose to believe in God's promise without testing to see if He would be faithful to fulfill it.

Satan tried one last temptation. He promised Jesus great kingdoms and offered them all to Jesus in exchange for worship. Basically, he was offering Jesus what God had already promised Him – that He would rule all the kingdoms of the world. But in Satan's offer, Jesus wouldn't have to go through death on the cross. Jesus once again turned to the Bible in His response, reminding Satan that Scripture says to worship and serve only God. He chose to trust God's plan, knowing that through His death, He would save the whole world.

Do you know what happened next? Read Matthew 4:11 and write it here:

_____

_____

_____

When Jesus told Satan to go, *he did*. So many people think of the devil as God's opposite – His equal. But he's not. He has no power against Jesus, and he has no power against you, either, if you refuse him. You don't have to feel afraid of him when you have Jesus. He will offer you the world and tell you what you want to hear...but there's always a catch. Don't fall for his lies. Stand firm on God's truth.

You can take comfort knowing that Jesus can relate to your struggles. He faced temptation and the same difficult emotions that you face. He knew anger. Sorrow. Exhaustion. Agony. There's nothing you will face today that He Himself hasn't faced, too. He's been there. He gets it. You can talk to Him, knowing He is listening and can relate.

Yes, Satan knows your weak spots. He will prey upon them. But even though God allows Satan to tempt you, He will always give you the strength to escape so you don't have to fall for it.

So how do you defend yourself? Well, notice what Jesus did every time Satan came at Him: He quoted Scripture. If Jesus used the Bible to defend Himself, shouldn't we? Take the time to memorize verses that speak to your struggles and God's promises. Write a short prayer to God, asking Him to help you recognize Satan's taunts and tricks so you won't fall for them. Ask Him to help you recognize your weaknesses and help you find Scripture that will speak to them to help you resist.

Day Twenty-Eight: Choose Your Friends Wisely

God wants a relationship with each one of us. He designed us in His image, giving us an inner desire to hang out with other people. The Bible encourages us to spend time together and help each other. Life can be so hard, and we were never meant to go through it alone. Read 1 Thessalonians 5:11 and write it here:

_____

_____

_____

_____

We are supposed to be there for each other. We are supposed to encourage others with our words and actions.

The Bible actually has advice for the kinds of friendships and relationships we should have. Who you hang out with matters. Read 1 Corinthians 15:33 and write it here:

_____

_____

_____

_____

If you choose to surround yourself with friends who encourage you to sin, you will fall. It's true. There's an old saying: "Show me your friends and I'll show you your future." We become like the people we spend the most time with – it's that simple. As soon as you began your walk with Jesus, you became a new creation. You can't keep running back to those old bad habits when you're made new. This doesn't mean you have to ditch your old friends completely and have nothing to do with them. But instead of putting yourself in situations that may tempt you to sin, invite them to hang out with you at church or a youth event.

The best way to stay on the path God designed for you is to surround yourself with people who will encourage you in your walk with God. Get connected with a youth group. Choose friends and boyfriends/girlfriends who will build you up and help you get closer to Jesus. Read Proverbs 13:20 and write it here:

_____

_____

_____

_____

Choosing your relationships wisely really is important. Don't assume you are strong enough to resist temptation and purposefully put yourself in situations that will cause you to sin. You will hear people make the argument that Jesus was a "friend of sinners." But Jesus never joined them in their sin. He met them as they were, but He didn't leave them there. He called them away from that life of sin.

Write a short prayer to God, asking Him to put the right people in your path. Ask Him to help you choose carefully and wisely when it comes to who you hang out with and who you date. Ask Him to help you become someone who encourages others and helps them walk closer to Him as well.

_____

_____

_____

_____

Day Twenty-Nine:
Who You're Working For

Have you ever rushed through something, just to get it done? It's tempting to do a job half-heartedly just to get it out of the way, especially when your to-do list seems never-ending. But God appreciates hard work. When He designed the Garden of Eden in the very beginning of the Bible – a beautiful, perfect place before sin entered – He gave Adam and Eve instructions to take care of it. He knows hard work is good for us, and He will never encourage you to give only half your effort. Read Colossians 3:23 and write it here:

_____

_____

_____

_____

Notice what it says: whatever job it is you have to do, do it for God…and not for men. It's really easy to fall into the trap of trying to impress others. But Jesus warned us not to do anything just to get praise or attention from others. You see it often in social media today – people who go out and do amazing things, like serving at a homeless shelter or giving money to people in need – only to video it and share it so others can tell them how awesome they are. If you are serving because it looks good and people will brag on you, your heart is in the wrong place. Do those good works, but do them quietly, letting your only motivation be to please God.

No matter what task is in front of you today, try doing it with a thankful heart. Changing your attitude will help you appreciate your life as a gift from God. Try just this small shift in your thinking: instead of saying you *have* to do that chore, say you *get* to. For example, you *get* to do the laundry, because it means you have clothes to wear. You *get* to do the dishes, because it means you had food to eat. Changing your mindset will help you make the most of whatever situation He has put you in.

You may feel like your role in this world is not very important, but God says it is. Everything you do can be done to glorify God. Even simple things like hanging out with friends or playing a sport. Even things you hate, like homework or studying or chores. When you're facing something difficult or something you really don't want to do, try telling God, *I am doing this for You.* It will help you stay focused on Him and accomplish anything that's in front of you.

Read the words of the Apostle Paul in 1 Corinthians 10:31 and write them here:

_____

_____

_____

_____

Give God your best efforts in whatever you do today – from the biggest responsibilities down to the smallest ones.

Write a short prayer to God, ask Him to help you with your mindset as you go about your day. Ask Him to help you do things for Him and not for others. Ask Him to help you keep a good attitude and work hard, even when you're doing the tasks you don't enjoy.

_____

_____

_____

_____

_____

_____

Day Thirty:
Loving the Least

Before we dig in today, let's start off with gratitude. What can you thank God for in your life today? Maybe it's a friend or family member. Maybe it's a special blessing He has given you this week. Whatever it is, thank Him for it.

_____

_____

_____

_____

Now, let's talk about love. So many people think love is something that just *happens*. Something you can't control. But the kind of love Jesus talked about is a very-much-on-purpose kind of thing. It takes action. It's not something you *have* but something you *do*.

Jesus described a day when He will come back into the world. All people, from every nation around the world, will be gathered to Him, and He will separate them. Some, He will welcome into His kingdom, saying, "I was hungry and you gave Me food, I was thirsty and you gave Me a drink, I was a stranger and you welcomed Me, I was naked and you clothed Me, I was sick and you visited Me, I was in prison and you came to Me" (Matthew 25:34-36). The people will be confused, wondering *when* they did any of those things for Jesus.

His reply will blow them all away. Read Matthew 25:40 and write it here:

_____

_____

_____

_____

Whatever we do for others, we do for Jesus. Loving Jesus goes beyond the walls of your church. It's reaching out to someone in need. It's giving of your own time and your own resources to do something for someone else – and not just for your friends and family. It's the kid who annoys you. It's the kid who isn't clean. It's the kid who lies or steals. It's the homeless on the streets. Jesus wants you to look beyond their appearance and their actions and see their hearts the way God sees them: souls who need His love and light.

So look around you. Do you see people in need? Are there people in your family or in your classes who could use something? Maybe it's the boy who is struggling by himself, without a friend to talk to. Maybe it's the girl who doesn't have a coat when it's cold and snowing. Can you be the one to reach out? If it will take money to fulfill the need, do you know where you could go to get it – maybe a teacher? Your youth leader?

The Bible says if we have the means to help in some way but choose not to even try, you're not letting the love of God fill you and work through you. Read 1 John 3:17 and write it here:

_____

_____

_____

_____

So go out into your world, asking God to help you see others through His eyes. Write a short prayer, asking Him to help you see the needs of others. Ask Him to give you the ability to provide those needs. Ask Him to help you share His love through your actions and your words. And remember, what you do for anyone in your path today, you do for Jesus.

_____

_____

_____

_____

Day Thirty-One: Judging Others

You've probably heard the expression, *Don't judge a book by its cover*. Yet, it's human nature to judge. We all do it. It's natural to make judgements about a person at first sight. It's natural to judge a person by the things they say and do. But Jesus has some pretty strong words about judging others. Read Matthew 7:1-2 and write those verses here:

_____

_____

_____

_____

If you really think about what He's saying in those verses, it's a little scary. The judgments you make against others will be the standard you are held to as well. Be honest with yourself. Are you guilty of making judgments about people in your school? Jesus promises you will be judged in the same way you judge others.

Don't get confused or misunderstand Jesus: sin is and will always be sin. You will see people in your life who are doing and saying things God doesn't like. Jesus isn't in anyway claiming that their sin is okay. What He *is* saying is that you shouldn't ignore the sin in your own life and focus on the people around you. Before you worry about the sins of those around you, take a good, hard look at yourself. Examine your own thoughts, words, and actions. Are they always pleasing to God? Or are there areas where you could use some improvement? Look *inside* before you start looking around. Just because they may sin in different ways than you do doesn't make them a "worse" person.

Someone once compared it to your favorite white T-shirt. When you pull that favorite T-shirt out of the closet and ask someone what color it is, they're going to say it's white, of course. If you hold it up against a red T-shirt, or a blue one, or any other color, it will always look white. But if you put it up against a brand new white T-shirt, one that's never been worn or washed, it's likely that favorite white T-shirt is going to look a little dingy. Maybe even slightly yellowed with age and wear.

Sin works like that favorite white T-shirt. It's easy to look at others and think, *Wow, I would never sin like he does*. I would never try drugs. Or drink. Or steal. Or *insert whatever sin you can think of here.* When you compare yourself to "bad" people, you may think of yourself as pretty good. But just because you aren't tempted by those sins, it doesn't mean you're perfect. In fact, when you examine yourself, you'll likely find some areas you need to work on, too.

Write a prayer to God, asking Him to help you fight your own sinful urges today. And when you do see sin all around you, ask Him to help you see those people through His eyes – as the people God created them to be. Ask Him to help you point them to Him in His loving way, rather than coming off as hateful and judgmental in what you say.

_____

_____

_____

_____

_____

_____

Day Thirty-Two: Relationship, Not Religion

Many people won't give Christianity a chance because they see it as following some list of rules. Be careful not to fall into that trap: being a Christian isn't about you and your performance. If you try to do it that way, you will fail. It's that simple. You can never live up to the perfection of Jesus, and when you fall short, you will get discouraged and feel like giving up. Getting caught up in the "following the rules" mentality is making it all about *religion*, when we've already discussed the fact that for God, it's about *relationship*. So what's the difference?

Religion is about going through a checklist of what you can and can't do. It's going through the motions each day. *I prayed this morning – check. I read my Bible before I went to bed – check. I didn't say anything mean today – check.* Don't get me wrong: that's all good stuff. God loves it when you pray and read your Bible. He loves it when you guard your words. But be careful not to see those things as just another item on your to-do list. Praying and reading the Bible was never meant to be a chore.

The religious leaders of Jesus's day, the Pharisees, dedicated their entire lives to this kind of religion. On the outside looking in, they were checking all the boxes. They memorized entire books of the Bible. They said long, elaborate prayers. They stayed far away from the "sinners." But they were going through the motions. Their hearts weren't truly seeking God. They followed their checklists and relied on themselves and their own behavior, thinking they could "earn" their way into heaven. They missed the whole point! When Jesus came to the world, they didn't even recognize Him as the Son of God. They're the very ones who put Him on that cross. They didn't recognize God when He was literally standing right in front of them.

Jesus wasn't afraid to call out the Pharisees for their religious behavior. Read Matthew 15:8 and write it here:

_____

_____

_____

_____

The Pharisees may have done and said the right things, but their hearts weren't in the right place. God wants your heart above everything else – when you give it to Him, the rest of that stuff will follow.

Relationship is seeking Jesus. It's recognizing you aren't and will never be good enough to do this on your own. It's coming to God because you love Him, not because it's on your to-do list. It's realizing that God doesn't love you because you've "earned" it somehow, but because He is good and loving.

Read Hosea 6:6 and write it here:

_____

_____

_____

_____

God wants your love above anything else you can offer Him. He wants you to trust Him to work in your life so that doing His will is your natural response, not a chore.

Write a prayer to God, asking Him to help you not to get sucked in to the spirit of *religion*. Ask Him to help you keep your heart in the right place – close to Him. Ask Him to help you focus on His love above everything else, so that following His will flows from your love for Him.

_____

_____

_____

_____

_____

_____

Day Thirty-Three: A Living Sacrifice

Do you ever feel like you're not worth much? If you ever start to doubt how important your life really is, remember the enormous price Jesus paid for you when He died on the cross and took on your sin. You are God's treasure! You are cherished by the One who created all things, and you belong to Him.

Because you are so important to Him, it matters to God how you take care of yourself. Read Romans 12:1-2 and write them here:

_____

_____

_____

_____

What does it mean to make your body a living sacrifice? It means knowing that as a follower of Jesus, the Spirit lives inside of you. It means protecting yourself from the pressures of the world, making choices that honor God. Everywhere you look, you will see the world has it all backwards when it comes to our bodies. You'll see skimpy clothing and provocative actions. But don't let the world fool you into thinking confidence is about showing off your body. Advertising your body for the world to see cheapens the beauty God gave you. Real confidence comes from within, from knowing you are loved and saved by Jesus.

Know this: you will be pressured to do things that don't honor God. That pressure may come in the form of drinking or using drugs. Not only do these substances harm your body, they alter your mind to a point that can cause you to make horrible, life-changing decisions. The pressure may come in the form of a boyfriend or girlfriend who wants you to give yourself to them before marriage, when God's plan is to wait until you have found your future husband or wife.

Read 1 Corinthians 6:19-20 and write it here:

_____

_____

_____

_____

No matter what form of pressure it is, imagine the Holy Spirit within you. *You are not your own.* Remembering this keeps it simple: if you wouldn't feel comfortable asking Jesus to participate in the action with you, it isn't honoring God. Saying "no" won't always be easy, and it won't be the popular choice. But your value does not come from the opinion of others. You have been chosen as one of His! Be proud of that. You are God's temple – give His Spirit a house that honors Him.

Write a short prayer to God, asking Him to help you honor Him with your actions. Ask Him to help you remember your body is a temple of His Spirit and to help you make choices that protect you from the world. It's okay to be real with God and tell Him where you struggle with this – He already knows it, anyway, and loves you just the same. Ask Him to help you remember your worth in His eyes and to treat your body with the value it deserves.

_____

_____

_____

_____

_____

_____

Day Thirty-Four:
Tell the World

If you saw someone walking straight into danger, what would you do? Say you saw someone about to step into oncoming traffic. Or maybe someone is about to walk into a burning building. Would you scream at him? Jump up and down and wave your arms? You would do whatever it took to get his attention, wouldn't you? You would never allow someone to walk into that kind of risk.

But what if you saw someone walking through this life without Jesus?

Remember that Jesus said He is the way to heaven. He didn't leave a to-do list of things you to do to get there; He said to believe in Him and what He did on the cross to take away your sins. When He called some of His first disciples – Simon-Peter and Andrew, who were fishing on the sea – He said something to them that applies to us, too. Read Matthew 4:19 and write it here:

_____

_____

_____

_____

"Fish" for people. What does that mean? It means we should always be looking for opportunities to share Jesus with the people in our path.

At the end of Jesus's time here on earth, after He had risen and appeared to so many, it was time for Him to take His place in heaven. Just before He left, He gave His disciples final instructions. Read Mark 16:15-16 and write those verses here:

_____

_____

Jesus wants everyone to have the chance to accept His salvation. All around you, you likely see people who don't know about Him – His love, His joy, His peace. What if *you* could be the reason someone gives his life to Jesus and goes to heaven someday? What if *one thing* you say or do introduces someone to the love of God?

Tell someone what Jesus has done in your life. Share what He did on the cross for all of us. Or simply invite someone to come to church or a youth event. If you let God work and speak through you, He can do some amazing things in the lives of others. Don't worry about what people will think. Don't stress out about what to say. Trust God to help you and let Him do what He does in the hearts of those who hear the message.

Write a short prayer to God, asking Him to help you "fish" for people. Ask Him to help you speak truth with love. Ask Him to give you the opportunities and the words to say. Finally, ask Him for courage and strength to share Jesus with the world.

Day Thirty-Five:
Be the Light

All around you, there are people who don't know about Jesus. People who have never accepted or maybe even never heard about His love and sacrifice. They walk in darkness, though they don't even realize it. Satan has covered the world in so much darkness that it's sometimes hard to even tell when you get lost in it.

But when Jesus is there, there is no darkness. Read John 8:12 and write it here:

_____

_____

_____

_____

He is the light of the whole world. When we walk with Him, we can't help but radiate His light as well. You can *light up* your homes, your classrooms, and everywhere else in your path simply by imitating Jesus and His love. Offer a smile and be kind when it's not easy. Choose joy, no matter what's going on around you.

Read this closely: You will never draw anyone to Jesus by being rude about their actions and their beliefs. You will not show them His incredible love by shouting how wrong they are and how right you are. The way to bring someone to Jesus is to show them His light: a light so amazing that they want it for themselves. Are you showing that light? Are you radiating His joy and peace so much that the people around you wish they had some of it, too? Because that's the key to introducing them to Jesus.

Write a short prayer to God, asking Him to help you show His light to someone who needs to see it today. Ask Him to help you light up the darkness around you and to let your words and actions reflect Him at all times.

Day Thirty-Six:
Stop Comparing Yourself to Others

Have you ever looked at someone and thought to yourself, *I wish I could be more like him?* Or, *I wish I had what she has?*

There are a lot of people out there with seemingly "perfect" lives. The people with money – expensive clothes and fancy things. The people who make straight A's with no effort. The people who are natural athletes. The popular people who everyone wants to be friends with. The people who look great every day, never having a bad hair day or a flaw on their skin.

The people who seem to have it all.

When you compare yourself to those "perfect" people around you, you're falling into a trap that leads to unhappiness and disappointment. Comparing yourself to anyone else is the ultimate thief of joy. Unfortunately, in today's world of social media, it's really easy to get caught up in the comparison game.

Remember: what you see on social media is basically an illusion. A highlight reel, if you will. Filtered, edited pictures that tell only a fraction of the real story – and sometimes, a totally made-up story. When you get caught up in the lives of others, wishing you were living like they are, you will be distracted from His peace. Every time you scroll and feel that twinge of jealousy, that little whisper telling you, *You will never be good enough…you will never measure up…*your joy shrinks a little bit more.

Don't compare yourself to anyone else. Read 2 Corinthians 10:12 and write it here:

_____

_____

_____

_____

When you find yourself feeling like you're not enough, stop looking around. Put down your phone. Focus on what's in front of you, the life God has blessed you with. Remember that YOU are created for a specific purpose, someone no one else can do the way you can. God created you and made a special plan for your life that won't look like anyone else's, and *that's amazing*.

Write a short prayer to God, asking Him to help you fix your thoughts on Him and not on comparing yourself to those around you. Ask Him to help you see the many blessings He has put in your path and not to get caught up in jealousy of others. Thank Him for creating a special path that's only for you and ask Him to help you follow it in His way, keeping your eyes on Him.

_____

_____

_____

_____

_____

_____

Day Thirty-Seven: God Knows You

Do you realize God had a plan for your life before you were ever born? So many people believe existence on this earth happens by chance, but the truth is, no life here is an accident. Read Psalm 139:13-14 and write those verses here:

_____

_____

_____

_____

_____

_____

"Fearfully and wonderfully made." On purpose, with special care. The Psalm goes on to say that even before God created you, He had already seen every single one of your days and what they would look like here on earth. He planned out your gifts and talents that would make you unique and amazing. Before you ever took your first breath in this world, God already had a plan for your whole life.

Your bond with God is unshakeable. He knows you so well – even better than you know yourself. After all, He made you! Read Psalm 139:1-2 and write those verses here:

_____

_____

_____

_____

_____

Every action you take – even those when you're all alone – God sees. In fact, this part of the Psalm goes on to say that before you even speak a word, He already knows what you're going to say. Before you think, He already knows your thoughts. And the beautiful part of all of that is this: He knows your flaws. He knows every mistake you have made and the mistakes you will make tomorrow. And despite all that, He loves you enough to give His life for you. You know you can trust Him with all you have and with all you are, because He *made* all you have and all you are.

Think about this: the God who created the entire universe actually spends His time thinking about you. Making plans for you. He even lives in you, guiding you in your path each day. Why ever doubt that your life doesn't have any worth? Why trust anyone besides Him, when He designed your days?

Write a short prayer to God, thanking Him for putting so much time and thought into you and your life. Thank Him for loving you more than you can ever understand. Ask Him to help you remember that no matter what the world says about you, you are "fearfully and wonderfully made" by Him.

Day Thirty-Eight:
God is Always Good

I bet you've heard the expression, *God is good.* It's a phrase that's often followed by, *All the time*. God is good, all the time. When someone is cured of cancer, God is good! When someone's needs are met in a miraculous way, God is good. He is always good – He is incapable of anything *but* good.

Read Psalm 145:9 and write it here:

_____

_____

_____

_____

He listens to our prayers. He showers us with blessings. He forgives us over and over and over again. Even when we're not, God is good.

So when life isn't good, what does that mean about God?

What about when the sickness wins? What about when a situation we've prayed about isn't resolved the way we hoped it would be?

Is God still good when the outcome is not?

We have to remember that we live in a broken world. Unfortunately, bad things happen…even to people who love God. The consequences of rampant sin affect us all. But remember to look at the life of Jesus. When He was here on earth, He endured everything we do today. When He lost his friend, He wept. He knew what it felt like to be hungry. He knew exhaustion. He didn't live a life of comfort or isolation – He went among the sick and needy, healing and offering His love and mercy. He endured humiliating mockery and beatings. Worst of all, He died a painful, demeaning death on the cross – a punishment reserved for the worst criminals – when He was completely innocent.

God knows troubles and heartache are part of the life you will experience here. He never promised to take all that pain away. He *did* promise something else, though. Read Deuteronomy 31:8 and write it here:

_____

_____

_____

_____

Whatever trouble you face, you are never alone. He goes before you and beside you, so you don't have to be afraid. He's willing to face the world with you, giving you the strength you need to get through anything life throws your way. Why? Because *He is good.*

Write a short prayer to God, just thanking Him for the good things He does in your life. Thank Him for being with you through the difficult times, and for giving you what you need to face your troubles.

_____

_____

_____

_____

_____

_____

Day Thirty-Nine: Doing the Impossible

Word spread quickly about Jesus and the miracles He did. As He gained popularity, fans began to follow Him, hoping to hear Him speak or see Him doing something amazing. In today's world, we would say he "went viral." Sometimes, thousands of people showed up when they knew He was going to be somewhere.

One day, after a full day spent with a huge multitude of people, evening began to set in. The disciples began to panic. They knew it was getting late, and in that location, there weren't a lot of options around for getting a meal to eat. They went to Jesus quietly and asked Him to send the people away, so they could go into the nearby villages and buy food.

But Jesus had other plans. He told the disciples the people didn't need to go anywhere...because they would feed the crowd themselves.

Can't you just imagine the disciples' faces? Picture a sold-out concert arena – that's the kind of crowd they had. Literally thousands of men, women, and children. And when they pooled their resources, they had five loaves of bread and two fish in their possession. How would they possibly feed them all?

The thing is, it was never about *what* they had. It was about *Who* they had with them. Jesus took that tiny amount of food and prayed, then let the disciples start passing it out to the huge crowds of people. Not only did they have enough to fill everyone's belly, they had twelve whole baskets of leftovers!

Read Jeremiah 32:17 and write it here:

_____

_____

_____

_____

Let's not get caught up in viewing our big problems through our own limited abilities. Keep it in perspective: the same God who literally just spoke the entire world into existence is working for you. How big does your problem seem when you put it up against the One who created all things?

It's easy to feel overwhelmed and ask God to send the problem away, just like the disciples did. But before you panic, try asking God to help you face the impossible – His way. Rely on Him to fill in the gaps where you fall short.

Write a short prayer, asking God to help you keep your faith in Him when it comes to facing your problems. Ask Him to help you remember how big He really is, and to help you remember that with Him, you can overcome even the most "impossible" situations.

_____

_____

_____

_____

_____

_____

Day Forty:
Real Friends

What qualities make someone a good friend? When you're choosing someone as a friend, what qualities do you look for in him or her?

_____

_____

_____

_____

Ask yourself an honest question: what qualities do *you* possess that make you a good friend to others? What could you do more of in order to be an even *better* friend?

When Jesus went to preach in Capernaum, many people came to the house where He stayed to hear Him. So many people showed up, there was no more room to come inside. But one group of men were determined to get their friend to Jesus.

Four men had heard about Jesus and the miraculous healings He had been doing. They knew if they could just get their paralyzed friend to Him, Jesus would heal this man so he could walk again.

But when they got to the house, they couldn't get inside. The crowd was huge and the door was blocked. There wasn't room to squeeze in someone else – especially not four men who were carrying someone lying on a bed. If this group was going to get to Jesus, they would have to get creative.

When they saw they weren't getting in the door, they climbed up to the clay roof of the house, carrying their friend along with them. The men dug into the roof until they made a hole in it. When the hole was big enough, they started lowering their paralyzed friend, along with his bed, into the home. Imagine the scene: all those people squeezed inside, and suddenly, a man starts coming down through a hole in the roof!

When Jesus saw the faith these men had in Him, He felt love and compassion for them. Not only did He heal the man so that he could get up and walk on his own for the first time in his life, He gave the man what he needed most of all – forgiveness of sins. When the man stood up, picked up his bed, and walked out of the room, the entire crowd watched in awe.

These men went to a lot of trouble to help a friend in need. Read Galatians 6:2 and write it here:

_____

_____

_____

_____

It's a calling to share in the problems of your friends. A calling to help in whatever way you can, even when it's not easy. It's about going out of your way to be there when a friend is in need.

The four men in this story proved their love for their friend by doing everything they could to get him to Jesus. You know it was difficult, carrying the man all that way…getting him up onto the roof…digging the hole and slowly lowering him into the house. It wasn't easy, but they didn't stop until they succeeded.

How can you be more like these four men, doing whatever it takes to help a friend in need? How can you go above and beyond to bring a friend to Jesus? Write a short prayer, asking God to help you be the kind of friend these men were, going above and beyond for the one they cared about.

_____

_____

_____

_____

About the Author

Katy Newton Naas spends much of her free time chasing her two young boys, three dogs, five cats, and eight ducks. She has published more than forty children's, young adult, and adult books, including YA Christian Book of the Year Award-winning novel, *Healing Rain*, and Literary Classics International Book Gold Award-winning novel, *Guardian*. She enjoys serving as youth leader in her church and teaching middle school reading and language arts in the local school system. Find her books at:

https://www.etsy.com/shop/BooksbyKNN.